A Note From Rick Renner

I am on a personal quest to see a "revival of the Bible" so people can establish their lives on a firm foundation that will stand strong and endure the test when end-time storm winds begin to intensify.

In order to experience a revival of the Bible in your personal life, it is important to take time each day to read, receive, and apply its truths to your life. James tells us that if we will continue in the perfect law of liberty — refusing to be forgetful hearers, but determined to be doers — we will be blessed in our ways. As you watch or listen to the programs in this series and work through this corresponding study guide, I trust you will search the Scriptures and allow the Holy Spirit to help you hear something new from God's Word that applies specifically to your life. I encourage you to be a doer of the Word He reveals to you. Whatever the cost, I assure you — it will be worth it.

> Thy words were found, and I did eat them;
> and thy word was unto me the joy and rejoicing of mine heart:
> for I am called by thy name, O Lord God of hosts.
> — Jeremiah 15:16

Your brother and friend in Jesus Christ,

Rick Renner

Overcoming Strife

Copyright © 2021 by Rick Renner
P.O. Box 702040
Tulsa, OK 74170

Published by Rick Renner Ministries
www.renner.org

ISBN 13: 978-1-68031-902-6

eBook ISBN 13: 978-1-68031-903-3

How To Use This Study Guide

This five-lesson study guide corresponds to *"Overcoming Strife" With Rick Renner* (Renner TV). Each lesson in this study guide covers a topic that is addressed during the program series, with questions and references supplied to draw you deeper into your own private study of the Scriptures on this subject.

To derive the most benefit from this study guide, consider the following:

First, watch or listen to the program prior to working through the corresponding lesson in this guide. (Programs can also be viewed at **renner.org** by clicking on the Media/Archive links.)

Second, take the time to look up the scriptures included in each lesson. Prayerfully consider their application to your own life.

Third, use a journal or notebook to make note of your answers to each lesson's Study Questions and Practical Application challenges.

Fourth, invest specific time in prayer and in the Word of God to consult with the Holy Spirit. Write down the scriptures or insights He reveals to you.

Finally, take action! Whatever the Lord tells you to do according to His Word, do it.

For added insights on this subject, it is recommended that you obtain Rick Renner's book *You Can Get Over It — How To Confront, Forgive, and Move On*. You may also select from Rick's other available resources by placing your order at **renner.org** or by calling 1-800-742-5593.

TOPIC

Give No Place to the Devil

SCRIPTURES

1. **Ephesians 4:26** — Be ye angry, and sin not: let not the sun go down upon your wrath.
2. **Ephesians 4:26** (*NLT*) — And "don't sin by letting anger control you." Don't let the sun go down while you are still angry.
3. **Ephesians 4:27** — Neither give place to the devil.

GREEK WORDS

1. "angry"— ὀργίζω (*orgidzo*): silent resentment that gives way to an outburst of emotion; deeply felt anger suddenly released; a swelling, growing wrathful emotion that explodes in rage
2. "wrath"— παροργίζω (*parorgidzo*): from παρά (*para*) and ὀργίζω (*orgidzo*); the word παρά (*para*) means alongside, and ὀργίζω (*orgidzo*): silent resentment that gives way to an outburst of emotion; deeply felt anger suddenly released; a swelling, growing wrathful emotion that explodes in rage; compounded, silent resentment or rage alongside of you
3. "give" — δίδωμι (*didomi*): give, allow, permit
4. "place" — τόπος (*topos*): a specific, marked-off, geographical location; an entry point; used to denote an opportunity
5. "devil" — διάβολος (*diabolos*): one who repetitiously strikes until successfully penetrating an object in order to ruin it, affect it, or take it captive; to slander, accuse, or defame; to penetrate by continuous assault; to ensnare with a net

SYNOPSIS

The five lessons in this study on **Overcoming Strife** will address the following topics:

- Give No Place to the Devil

- Identifying Entry Points for Strife
- The Tongue, a Releaser of Strife
- The Demonic Source of Strife
- How To Put an End to Strife

The emphasis of this lesson:

The devil is always looking for a way to penetrate your life. He wants to find a way to gain access into every relationship you have and spoil it. And just like a watchman who guards and protects the borders or gates of a property or building, you have to stand at the entrance of your life and say, "No admittance!" This lesson will explain the importance of declaring and enforcing your life to be a "No Strife Zone" and examine the consequences if you don't.

An Outburst of Strife Exploded Into Revolution and a Devastating Civil War

In 1917, the Winter Palace in Saint Petersburg, Russia, was the site of major strife. The Tsar abdicated on the first of March. His title went to his brother who also abdicated. The Romanovs no longer wanted to rule Russia. Therefore, the leadership of the nation went to a provisional government that moved into the Winter Palace and settled there for several months.

It was a very difficult time for Russia. During that period, Vladimir Lenin began to plan his coup against the provisional government. It was about 9:00 p.m. on October 25 that the first revolutionaries came to the Winter Palace. They attempted to penetrate the palace through a monumental ornamental gate, but they were stopped by the guards working inside the palace. But this horrible strife eventually led to the penetration of the palace several hours later, which then led to the Russian Civil War which lasted from 1917 until 1922, in which millions and millions of people perished.

In Ephesians 4:26 and 27, the Apostle Paul wrote, "Be ye angry, and sin not: let not the sun go down upon your wrath. Neither give place to the devil." The word "angry" here is the Greek word *orgidzo*, and it depicts *a silent resentment that gives way to an outburst of emotion. It is a deeply felt anger that is suddenly released; a swelling, growing wrathful emotion that explodes in rage.* Paul was warning us about rage and urging us to not let rage get the best of us.

What did the apostle Paul mean by the statement, "Be ye angry and sin not and let not the sun go down upon your *wrath?*" (Ephesians 4:26) The Greek word for "wrath" is *parorgidzo*, a compound word from the word *para*, meaning *alongside*, and *orgidzo*, the Greek word for *angry*. Again, the word "angry" depicts *a silent resentment that gives away to an outburst of emotion.* It is *a deeply felt anger that is suddenly released; a swelling, growing wrathful emotion that explodes in rage.*

But when you compound the word *para* and the word *orgidzo*, it depicts *a silent resentment or rage that is alongside of you.* You go to bed with it like it is your partner. If you're married, this is extremely troublesome because it means there's going to be something between you and your spouse. That thing between you and your spouse is wrath — it is resentment, it is unforgiveness, it is rage — and it separates you from that person you love.

Whether you're married or not, the Bible says you're not to go to bed with resentment and rage as your partner. Do not go to bed in this attitude. Rick and Denise made a commitment years ago that they would not go to bed if they had a problem with one another. They determined that they would work it out because they didn't want anything to get between them.

In Ephesians 4:27, Paul went on to say, "Neither give place to the devil." That's powerful. This means that anger and rage gives place to the devil and opens a door for strife. And in this verse, Paul says, "Neither *give* place...." The word "give" is a form of the Greek word *didomi*, which means *to give, to allow, or to permit.* This means there are things *we* do that give the devil permission to find a place in our relationships.

Continuing in this verse, Paul said, "Neither give *place....*" The word "place" is the Greek word *topos*, which describes *a specific marked-off geographical location* — a real place. It is *an entry point*, and it depicts *an opportunity.* When you're wrathful — when you're angry and filled with rage and strife — and you don't resolve it, it literally opens a real door, just as real as any door to your house.

And when the door is open, the enemy finds an access point to enter your life. It becomes an opportunity for the devil; it gives "...place to the devil" (Ephesians 4:27). The word "devil" is the Greek word *diabolos.* And although we use the word *diabolos* as *a name,* the word "devil," translated from the Greek word *diabolos,* really is his *job description.*

Diabolos is a compound of two words — *dia* and *ballo.* The first word, *dia,* carries the idea of *penetration.* The second word, *ballo,* means *to throw something like a ball or a rock.* But when you compound these two words, it literally describes *one who repeatedly strikes and strikes and strikes until he successfully penetrates an object in order to ruin it, affect it, or to take it captive.*

The word "devil" — the Greek word *diabolos* — also means *to slander, accuse, or defame.* It denotes *penetration by continuous assault,* or *to ensnare with a net.* You always know when the devil has found access because the way you think begins to be affected. Rather than thinking positively about the person you love, you begin to see and highlight every flaw and defect in their personality. When strife has entered, all you see is what you don't like about your loved one because the defamer, the slanderer, has gone to work in your mind and in your emotions to point out everything bad in that other person.

When you begin to think like this, it's evident that the devil has found an access point into your mind and your emotions. And very often you become ensnared, almost as if ensnared in a net. Think of a strife-filled moment in your life when you were involved in a wrangling conversation with someone that was so unpleasant it seemed you couldn't find your way out of that conversation. You were ensnared because the devil had found access to that moment in your life.

A Testimony of the Horrible Consequences of Strife

On the program, Rick shared a personal experience with strife:

"I have a testimony from my life that demonstrates the horrible results of strife entering a situation. Many, many years ago, Denise and I were traveling in a very small car across the United States to preach in meetings. The car was so small we didn't even have room in our trunk for our luggage, so I tied it to the top of the car. Our son Paul was in the back seat. We had so much stuff in the back seat, sometimes we would have to look to make sure Paul was really back there. Philip was a newborn, so Denise was carrying Philip on her lap.

"Well, cramped quarters like that can quickly present an opportunity for disagreement and strife. Paul wouldn't stay in his car seat, so I was constantly wrangling with Paul trying to get him to stay in his car seat. He would climb out, and I would pull the car over to put him back in his car seat. By the time I would get back in my seat, Paul was already out of his car seat again. Then Philip would start crying. We were driving for hours and hours and hours from one church to another church, from one state to another state.

"One day very late in the evening, Denise and I got in strife. To be honest, it's very unusual for Denise and me to get into strife. We're just not strifeful people. But that evening while driving down the road we got into strife. While we were in strife something terrible happened. I had a piping-hot cup of coffee in the coffee holder between me and Denise. And in that strifeful moment, Philip reached over from Denise's lap and put his hand into that cup of coffee. Well, of course, it burned his little hand, but we didn't realize how badly he was burned because we were driving late at night and the car was dark. He cried and cried, and his crying became worse and worse.

"Finally, we pulled the car over and turned on the light. When we looked, we couldn't believe what we saw. That coffee was so hot that when Philip put his tiny hand into that coffee, it melted the skin from the bottom of his hand. The skin had slipped down from the bottom of his hand and it was lying on his arm. It was *horrible*.

"We rushed to an emergency room where they treated him. They had to take scissors and cut off all that skin and wrap his hand. They instructed us that while we were on that trip, every single day we had to find an emergency room where they could treat Philip's hand.

"For the next 30 days as we traveled across the country, we went to hospital emergency rooms every day so they could trim the dead skin and treat Philip's hand. Denise and I understood that if we had not been in a spirit of strife that would not have happened to Philip. Strife is a door opener that gives place to the devil to do evil things. Denise and I made a decision then that we would have a no-strife policy in our lives and keep the door shut to the devil."

Anger and Rage Resulted in Complete Humiliation

On the program, Rick then shared about an incident that happened in their lives that was caused by allowing anger and rage to enter a situation:

"Later, there was another moment when I got into strife. By this time we were living in the former Soviet Union. It was summer, and I had been invited to preach in Europe. So I said to Denise, 'Let's go to Europe and take our boys. It will be a wonderful experience for them to travel and to see these churches in Europe.'

"So the day came for us to go to the airport. Denise was taking too long to get ready, and the boys were not serious about getting packed and getting into the car. I became frustrated. My frustration turned into anger, then it turned into rage and I began yelling: 'Get in the car! If you don't get into the car, I'm going to go on this trip without you!' I was in a spirit of full-blown rage.

"That week, a friend was going to stay in our home with her dog so she could take care of our dog while we were gone. Well, when I got into that spirit of strife I yelled, 'Fine! I'm going to load this luggage into the car by myself, and if you're not in the car in minutes I'm headed to the airport by myself!'

"So in a fit of anger, I opened the front door to take that luggage out to the car, and when I did, our administrator's dog ran out the front door and got into a fight with our dog, which was a massive St. Bernard.

"I remember thinking, *Ugh, wonderful… we need to go to the airport and now our dog is going to kill our administrator's dog!* So I ran down to the driveway and stood between the dogs just as our dog put his jaws around the neck of the other dog. Without thinking, which is often what you do when you're in a spirit of strife — you don't think right, I reached my hands into the jaws of our St. Bernard to pull it off the other dog. And when I did, our dog chomped on the other dog, but he also chomped on my finger. And when he did, he bit off the end of my finger!

"Now I'm standing in our driveway with blood pouring from my finger. I walked up to the house and into the bathroom to wash my finger under the faucet and begin to wrap it with toilet tissue. I walked into the entryway as Denise came down the stairs, finally ready to get into the car. I said, 'Denise, the dog just bit off the end of my finger.' Denise said, 'Oh Rick, that's not a funny joke.' I said, 'You're right. It's not!' Then, I showed her my hand.

"Rather than go to the airport, Denise and I then got in the car and drove to the hospital, which was a very old Soviet-style hospital. And when they saw my finger, they checked me in as a patient and told me I had to stay all night in the hospital. The condition of the hospital was so terrible. The tiles were broken and falling off the walls. As we walked down the hallway to my room, we had to wave the cigarette smoke out of the way.

"When I finally reached my room and got into my bed, I looked at my surroundings and there was a single light bulb hanging on a little wire from the ceiling. There was a sink in my room hanging lopsided on one screw. The doctors and the nurses began giving me shots. And the next day they said, 'Mr. Renner, we need to tell you that there's a law in this country that if your dog has not had a rabies shot then you have to have rabies shots. Has your dog had a rabies shot?' 'No,' I said. 'But it's our dog, and I know that our dog doesn't have rabies.'

"He said, 'Unfortunately that means, by law, *you have to have rabies shots.*'

"Well, that day they were giving me shots in my arm and my bottom. Just giving me all kinds of shots and trying to treat me and stop this bleeding. And he finally said, 'Mr. Renner, we're going to let you go with your children and your family to Europe to do your meetings, but we need to tell you something. These rabies shots are very serious. There are seven all together, and if you fail to take one of these rabies shots on time you will get rabies from these shots. So as you travel, we're going to give you the syringes and the medication, and you will have to find someone in every location to give you the rabies shot, or you will get rabies.'

"I remember lying in my bed thinking of the movie *Old Yeller* — how Old Yeller developed rabies and they had to chain the dog to a tree. I could just see myself foaming at the mouth because I didn't take my rabies shot on time! So I took the solution and the syringes with Denise and the boys and our luggage. We went to the airport and flew to Europe with my finger all wrapped up. In every church we went to I was humiliated when I had to ask every pastor if he happened to have a nurse in the church who could give me a rabies shot.

"I was sure they wondered what kind of speaker was I? The *speaker* needs a rabies shot! And church after church, the nurse would come into the pastor's office and would say, 'Mr. Renner, pull down your pants and we'll give you a shot.' I was about to preach the Bible in these churches — even to the very person giving me the shot in my bottom. I was humiliated.

"Church after church, we went through this pattern — pulling my pants down for a nurse in every church with Denise at my side so I could get a rabies shot in total, complete humiliation. And the Holy Spirit kept saying to me all along the way, *If you had not gotten into strife, the door would have never been opened for this.* Finally we came home, and I had one more rabies shot to take so I went to the hospital emergency room. They said, 'Mr. Renner, it's good to see you. Step behind the curtain to get ready for your last shot.'

"So I went behind the curtain and pulled my pants down, just as I'd done in all those churches all over Europe. When the nurse came behind the curtain and looked at me, she said, 'Mr. Renner what are you doing? We give these shots *in the arm*.' I had pulled my britches down in churches all over Europe when I didn't have to because the shot was supposed to be given in the arm.

"But you see, I was in the spirit of strife when those injections were first given to me. I couldn't hear correctly. When you get into a spirit of strife you don't think right, you don't act right, and you don't hear right. As a result, you can set yourself up for unnecessary difficulty or humiliation. Strife becomes an entry point for the enemy to find his way into your environment. And that is why the apostle Paul says don't give the devil any place in your life."

In our next lesson, we will identify entry points for strife and learn how to close the door to overcome strife.

STUDY QUESTIONS

**Study to shew thyself approved unto God, a workman that needeth
not to be ashamed, rightly dividing the word of truth
— 2 Timothy 2:15**

1. The word "angry" in the Greek is the word *orgidzo*, which depicts a silent resentment that gives way to an outburst of emotion. This deeply felt anger grows into wrathful emotion that explodes in rage. Nothing good can come from such an outburst. What detailed guidance is given in Ephesians 4:25-27?

2. The meaning of the Greek word for "devil" is the actual job description of demonic operations: repeatedly striking to gain access until successfully penetrating a life or relationship in order to ruin it or to take it captive. What scriptures do you rely upon personally to shield your life against such attacks?

3. In Rick's humorous telling of his "rabies-shot" story, what serious lesson did you learn regarding the painful and humiliating consequences of strife?

PRACTICAL APPLICATION

**But be ye doers of the word, and not hearers only,
deceiving your own selves.
— James 1:22**

1. Can you recall an instance when you "gave place" to anger and strife? What was the result? How did you remedy the situation and what did you learn from it?

2. When strife enters a relationship, all you can see is what you don't like about the other person because the defamer and slanderer has gone to work in your mind and in your emotions. Are you currently experiencing difficulty with a person in your life? What is the root cause of the conflict? Have you determined how the devil was given access to that relationship? What do you plan to do to shut the door and prevent him from roaming to find additional access?

3. Can you recall a situation in your own life when strife caused harm to an innocent person? How was the situation and relationship restored?

TOPIC

Identifying Entry Points for Strife

SCRIPTURES

1. **Ephesians 4:26** — Be ye angry, and sin not: let not the sun go down upon your wrath.

2. **Ephesians 4:26** (*NLT*) — And don't sin by letting anger control you. Don't let the sun go down while you are still angry

3. **Ephesians 4:27** — Neither give place to the devil.

4. **Ephesians 4:29** — Let no corrupt communication proceed out of your mouth, but that which is good to the use of edifying, that it may minister grace unto the hearers.

5. **Ephesians 4:30** — And grieve not the holy Spirit of God, whereby ye are sealed unto the day of redemption.

6. **Ephesians 3:31** — Let all bitterness, and wrath, and anger, and clamour, and evil speaking, be put away from you, with all malice.

7. **Ephesians 4:32** — And be ye kind one to another, tenderhearted, forgiving one another, even as God for Christ's sake hath forgiven you.

GREEK WORDS

1. "angry" — ὀργίζω (*orgidzo*): silent resentment that gives way to an outburst of emotion; deeply felt anger suddenly released; a swelling, growing wrathful emotion that explodes in rage

2. "wrath" — παροργίζω (*parorgidzo*): from παρά (*para*) and ὀργίζω (*orgidzo*); the word παρά (*para*) means alongside, and ὀργίζω (*orgidzo*); silent resentment that gives way to an outburst of emotion; deeply felt anger suddenly released; a swelling, growing wrathful emotion that explodes in rage; compounded, silent resentment or rage alongside of you

3. "give" — δίδωμι (*didomi*): give, allow, permit

4. "place" — τόπος (*topos*): a specific, marked-off, geographical location; an entry point; used to denote an opportunity

5. "devil" — διάβολος (*diabolos*): one who repetitiously strikes until successfully penetrating an object in order to ruin it, affect it, or take it captive; to slander, accuse, or defame; to penetrate by continuous assault; to ensnare with a net

6. "corrupt" — σαπρός (*sapros*): putrid or rotten; depicts something that is disgusting to taste or repulsive to smell; describes anything that is rank, foul, putrid, rotten, corrupt, or worthless; something nasty

7. "communication" — λόγος (*logos*): a single word

8. "good" — ἀγαθός (*agathos*): anything good, beneficial, or profitable; describes that which is brave or noble

9. "edifying" — οἰκοδομή (*oikodome*): an architectural term meaning to enlarge or amplify a house; to edify; to improve; to leave in an improved condition

10. "grieve" — λύπη (*lupe*): denotes pain or grief; depicts shock, devastation, hurt, wounds, and grief; depicts something that is painful, sorrowful, filled with anguish, torment, or agony; depicts the emotions felt when spousal unfaithfulness occurs

11. "bitterness" — πικρία (*pikria*): an inner bitterness or attitude toward someone, toward a group, or toward a situation; inner poison that causes one to eventually become unkind, sour, sharp, sarcastic, scornful, cynical, mocking, contemptuous, and wounding

12. "wrath" — θυμός (*thumos*): portraying a person who suddenly flares up and loses control; deep-seated anger; an outburst; a person who boils over with anger and blows up, erupting in an ugly outburst that negatively affects other people

13. "anger" — ὀργίζω (*orgidzo*): silent resentment that gives way to an outburst of emotion; deeply felt anger suddenly released; a swelling, growing wrathful emotion that explodes in rage

14. "clamour" — κραυγή (*krauge*): uncontrollable outbursts; yelling; screaming

15. "evil speaking" — βλασφημία (*blasphemi*): to speak derogatory words for the purpose of injuring or harm; any derogatory speech that defames, injures, or harms another person; debasing, derogatory, nasty, shameful, ugly speech that humiliates someone

16. "be put away" — **αἴρω** (*airo*): away; pruned; an intentional putting away

17. "malice" — **κακός** (*kakos*): a vicious disposition; one who acts in spite

18. "be ye" — **γίνομαι** (*ginomai*): become; indicates progression

19. "kind" — **χρηστός** (*chrestos*): helpfulness; warm-heartedness; a willingness to show goodness from the heart to others; pictures a person who is attentive to the needs of others; one who is considerate of other people and their needs; compassionate, considerate, sympathetic, humane, kind, and gentle; when applied to interhuman relationships, it conveys the idea of being adaptable to others

20. "tenderhearted" — **εὔσπλαγχνος** (*eusplagchnos*): tender emotions; to be deeply moved to take some type of helpful action

21. "forgiving" — **χαριζόμενοι** (*charidzomenoi*): literally, gracing

22. "forgiven" — **ἐχαρίσατο** (*echarisato*): literally, has graced

SYNOPSIS

On October 25, 1917, revolutionaries tried to penetrate the gate of the Winter Palace in Saint Petersburg, Russia. Although they were stopped by the guards who kept them outside, they weren't deterred — they were determined to make another attempt to gain access into the palace.

This grievous moment in the history of Russia led to a revolution, which ultimately led to the Russian Civil War in which millions and millions of people died. In fact, to this day no one is sure how many people died in that Civil War. But the widespread mayhem and murder which ensued all began with a single act of strife. In penetrating a natural gate, revolutionaries opened wide a door to the destructiveness of strife, which unleased every evil work.

In the same manner, our words and actions can open a door for strife to enter and bring devastation beyond anything we could ever imagine. For this reason, we must guard against strife and learn to detect how strife can gain access to our lives so we can shut the door to the devil in every area and relationship. Years ago Denise and I understood that strife was an entry point for the work of the enemy into our lives and into our family, so we made a no-strife policy, and it closed the door to strife. You can do this, too.

The emphasis of this lesson

Ephesians 4:27 tells us to give no place to the devil and then immediately lists attitudes including bitterness, unforgiveness, quarreling, and strife. These attitudes are not only door openers for the devil, but they also grieve the Holy Spirit when we allow them to gain access into our relationships. It is vitally important to keep the devil out of our relationships. This lesson will explain how to identify entry points that allow strife into our lives. You will also learn how to kick strife out of your life so you can restore peace, order, and civility again.

Close All Specific Entry Points for Strife!

In Ephesians 4:27, the apostle Paul wrote, "Neither give place to the devil." The word translated "give" is a form of the Greek word *didomi*, which means *to give, to allow,* or *to permit.* So you could translate this verse, "Neither allow place to the devil" or "Neither permit place to the devil" which means *our* actions open doors for the enemy to find access to our lives.

The apostle Paul was clear in saying that we must stop allowing the devil to gain access. In Greek, the word "place" in Ephesians 4:27 is the word *topos,* which describes *a specific, marked-off geographical location.* In fact, it's where we get the term for a topographical map. The word *topos* means a specific marked-off place that the devil finds as *an entry point.* It can also be defined as *an opportunity* — which the enemy will most assuredly take.

Wrong attitudes or actions open doors, providing an opportunity for the devil to access us. As we've already seen, the word "devil" is the Greek word *diabolos,* which pictures *one who repetitiously strikes and strikes and strikes until he successfully penetrates an object in order to ruin it, affect it, or to take it captive.* In this verse, the word "devil" is more of a job description than it is a name.

That's what the devil does through strife — he affects relationships; he ruins relationships; he takes those relationships captive. But the word "devil" also means *to ensnare with a net.* And very often when you find yourself in strife, suddenly you're in the midst of a conversation so deep you feel you've been ensnared — you don't even know how you got there, and you don't know how to get out. That is evidence that the devil has found his way into your relationship or into a conversation.

But how do you identify things that open the door for strife? Let's consider what Paul wrote in Ephesians 4:29, which says, "Let no corrupt communication proceed out of your mouth, but that which is good to the use of edifying, that it may minister grace unto the hearers."

Corrupt communication is an entry point that the devil uses to access relationships. You may wonder, *What does "corrupt communication" mean? Does that mean curse words?* No. Christians don't use curse words, but Christians do speak corrupt communication.

The word "corrupt" is the Greek word *sapros*. The word *sapros* describes something that is *putrid or rotten*. It depicts *something that is disgusting to taste or repulsive to smell*. And it *describes anything that is rank, foul, putrid, rotten, corrupt, or worthless; something that is nasty*.

Paul continued his admonition in Ephesians by saying, "Let no corrupt *communication* proceed out of your mouth...." The word "communication" is the Greek word *logos*, which describes *a single word*. This means *a single word* can bring something putrid into a conversation. *One word* can open the door for something rotten and nasty to come into a relationship. And the apostle Paul knew that. That's why he said to not give place to the devil (*see* Ephesians 4:27), and then identified corrupt communication as one of the door openers for strife.

This verse continues, "...But that which is *good* to the use of edifying...." The word "good" is the Greek word *agathos*, which describes *anything good or beneficial or profitable*. It describes *something that is brave or noble*. So you can gauge yourself through self-evaluation. Ask yourself: "Are my words pleasant, or are they negative and nasty? Are my words encouraging and edifying, or rotten and putrid? Do my words leave people feeling as though they need to take a shower when I leave them? Or are my words brave and noble? Do the words I speak produce something good in the hearers?"

In fact, Ephesians 4:29 says our words should be spoken "to the use of edifying." The word "edifying" is the Greek word *oikodome*, and it is *an architectural term which means to enlarge or to amplify a house; to edify, to improve, or to leave in an improved condition*. When people talk with you, do they feel as though they have been slimed or do they feel they have been improved? We should make it our intention that our words leave every listener feeling better because they had a conversation with us. Our words should always "minister grace unto the hearers."

But the apostle Paul told us that corrupt communication — verbiage that is negative — includes gossip, backbiting, and all kinds of horrible behaviors. Corrupt, negative communication opens the door wide to strife in our relationships. Ask yourself: "Am I making room for corrupt communication?" If so, you need to stop immediately and close that door.

Bitterness Is a Deadly 'Door Opener' for Strife

Paul went on to say in Ephesians 4:30, "And *grieve* not the holy Spirit of God, whereby ye are sealed unto the day of redemption." The word "grieve" is from the Greek word *lupe*, which denotes *pain or grief*. It depicts *shock, devastation, and hurt*, and *filled with anguish, torment, or agony*. Corrupt communication not only opens a door for strife, but it also *grieves* the Holy Spirit.

But that's not all. In Ephesians 4:31, Paul added, "Let all *bitterness*, and wrath, and anger, and clamour, and evil speaking, be put away from you, with all malice."

This verse is loaded. The first thing Paul mentions is "bitterness." That lets us know that bitterness is a door opener for the enemy. Bitterness is the deadly root for many "door openers" for strife, and its danger is revealed by the meaning of the word bitterness. The word "bitterness" is the Greek word *pikria*, which depicts *an inner bitterness or attitude toward someone or toward a group, or toward a situation*. It is *an inner poison* that causes one to eventually become unkind, sour, sharp, sarcastic, scornful, caustic, cynical, mocking, contemptuous, and wounding in his words and in his behavior.

God has called you to live at a higher level than that, and when you sink to that level of communication it opens the door for strife to come. Then in Ephesians 4:31, Paul mentions wrath. The word "wrath" is the Greek word *thumos*, which portrays a person who suddenly flares up and loses his control as a result of some kind of unresolved, deep-seated anger. It describes a person who boils over with anger and blows up, erupting in an ugly outburst that negatively affects other people. And the apostle Paul says this is a door opener that gives place to the enemy.

So far, we've seen that corrupt communication — bad language, speaking negative things that are just putrid (such as gossip and back-biting) — opens the door for strife. Furthermore, corrupt communication also grieves the Holy Spirit. Now we've also seen that bitterness is an inner poison that causes you to be sharp, caustic, sour, cynical; it opens a door for strife.

Ephesians 4:31 continues, "Let all bitterness, and wrath, and *anger*, and clamour…" The word "anger" is the Greek word *orgidzo*, which we saw in the last lesson, describes *a silent resentment that gives way to an outburst of emotion*. It denotes *a deeply felt anger that is suddenly released*. It also expresses *a swelling, growing, wrathful emotion that explodes in rage*. Anger devastates others, it opens the door for hurt, and it opens the door for a spirit of strife. Regarding anger, Paul urged to "put away from you."

Paul then included "clamour" in this list of wrong actions and attitudes. The word "clamour" is the Greek word *krauge*, which describes *uncontrollable outbursts; yelling and screaming*. Demonic activity can fester in this kind of flesh-fueled atmosphere. My friends, you are higher than that. There's no room for yelling and screaming in your life — you have the Spirit of God in you! When you have a carnal outburst, yelling and screaming, it not only opens the door for strife, but it also gives the enemy footing for all kinds of wounding in people's lives. Put away clamor — put it far away from you.

The apostle Paul then proceeded to mention "evil speaking" in Ephesians 4:31. What is "evil speaking"? In Greek, it is the word *blasphemi*, and it's where we get the word *blasphemy*. Many people think that blasphemy is "blaspheming the divine" or "blaspheming God," but in fact, the word *blasphemi* — translated here as "evil speaking" — means *to speak derogatory words for the purpose of injuring or harm*. It is *any derogatory speech that defames, injures, or harms another person*.

This word *blasphemi* depicts *debasing, derogatory, nasty, shameful, sarcastic, ugly speech that humiliates someone*. Our words should never be used to humiliate another person. Even if there's something that you don't appreciate in others, you don't have to assault them with words and humiliate them.

The Spirit of God lives within you. Your words should reflect His words and His ways. Because of His indwelling presence, you have the capacity to speak divinely inspired words that minister grace to those who hear you. And your words should leave them in an improved condition. If you're humiliating people with your words, you are opening the door for the spirit of strife to enter and hurt you, as well as those subjected to your harmful words. So, refrain from humiliating, derogatory speech. In fact, the apostle Paul says such evil speaking should be "…put away from you."

"Put away" in Greek is *airo*, and it describes *a pruning or an intentional cutting away*. You have to make the decision to *not* speak this way to anyone in any situation.

Finally, Ephesians 4:31 concludes, "Let all bitterness, and wrath, and anger, and evil speaking, be put away from you, with all *malice*." In addition to putting away bitterness, wrath, anger, and evil speaking, we are to put away "malice." The word "malice" is the Greek word *kakos*, which depicts *a vicious disposition* or *one who acts in spite*. Malice is the desire to inflict injury, harm, or suffering on another, either because of a hostile impulse or out of deep-seated meanness. Don't allow a root of bitterness to produce malicious, spiteful behavior in your life. It will only defile others and open a door for strife.

Open the Right Doors!

Instead of opening doors for strife, make a decision to close some doors instead. In Ephesians 4:32, the apostle Paul gives us a list of "door closers" that will shut out strife every time. Instead of speaking hurtful negative words, we are to "...be ye kind one to another, tenderhearted, forgiving one another, even as God for Christ's sake hath forgiven you."

When you're tempted to fly off the handle and erupt into rage, whatever your flesh wants to yell at that point is *sapros* — corrupt — it's vile, it's putrid, and it's rotten. So instead of giving place to that — refrain. Just refrain by choosing to prune those negative attitudes. When you close that door, choose to open the door for kindness instead.

Ephesians 4:32 begins, "And *be ye*...." It's very interesting that in Greek "be ye" is *ginomai*, a form of the Greek word *ginomi*, which *indicates progression*. This means you may not attain that type of response immediately, but you have to start where you are. It could be translated "and be ye being kind by beginning the process where you are now." You have *to start where you are*. You won't obtain perfection immediately but begin where you are and by being kind to others.

The word "kind" is the Greek word *chrestos*, which describes *helpfulness; warm-heartedness;* and *a willingness to show goodness from the heart to others*. It is a decision to take a helpful position rather than being an enemy or an adversary. It pictures *a person who is attentive to the needs of others, one who is considerate of other people and their needs*. It depicts one that is compassionate, considerate, sympathetic, humane, kind, and gentle. And when applied to inter-human relationships it conveys the idea of being adaptable to others.

Rather than demand that others become like you, you'll begin to look for ways that you can change or adapt so that you can become a help to them. Instead of insisting that they meet your requirements, you begin to see how you can be compassionate and helpful to them. When you set yourself to respond with kindness in situations, you will position yourself to be an open door for the goodness of God to be released through you.

Paul then said we are to be "kind to one another, *tenderhearted....*" The word "tenderhearted" is a very unusual Greek word — *eusplagchnos*, and it describes *tender emotions*, or *to be deeply moved to take some kind of helpful action*. So, rather than be caustic and cynical you make a decision to be tenderhearted. How can you be positive? How can you be helpful? One way you can demonstrate tenderheartedness is "...forgiving one another, even as God for Christ's sake has forgiven you" (Ephesians 4:32).

The word "forgiving" is the Greek word *charidzomenoi*, from the root word *charis*, which is the word for "grace." The Greek literally says *gracing one another*. You may think they don't deserve forgiveness. Maybe they don't, but neither did we. You can *grace* them with what they don't deserve — just as God for Christ's sake graced us with forgiveness. The Greek communicates it clearly: "Even as God for Christ's sake has *graced* you." God did not have to forgive you. God knew everything about you; He knew everything you did, and He knew everything that you would do. But God, for Christ's sake, made a decision to grace you. He graced you for Christ's sake.

'Grace' Others — *Even As* God 'Graced' You!

And the same way that God has graced you, you are now in a position where you can grace someone else. Maybe they're not doing what you wish they would do. Maybe you think their behavior is lower than it ought to be. But rather than get into a spirit of strife with them you can tell yourself, *How would God deal with this? How has God dealt with me? Well, He's graced me, He's been patient with me, and He continues to work with me. And in the same way that God has graced me, I have the opportunity to grace this individual.*

When you take that position, you close the door to strife. If you take the alternative position where you blow up and fly into a fit of rage, you will open the wrong door! You'll begin to speak things that are putrid and negative. As a result, you will open every door for a spirit of strife to come into your life and to come into that relationship.

But when you take a different position by reversing your behavior you will give place to tenderhearted compassion. That's a door that God will walk through, and the devil cannot enter. When you make the decision to do everything you can to be helpful and warmhearted, you have just closed the door to the enemy, and you can overcome a spirit of strife.

In our next lesson, we will study how the tongue is a "releaser of strife."

STUDY QUESTIONS

Study to shew thyself approved unto God, a workman that needeth not to be ashamed, rightly dividing the word of truth.
— 2 Timothy 2:15

1. How does the Bible define "corrupt communication"? List three scriptures that give specific instruction about your words.

2. The word "forgiving" is a form of the Greek word *charis*, which is the word for "grace." In Ephesians 4:32, the Greek literally says, "gracing one another." How do you observe grace (and the consequences of withholding it) as described in the passage of Matthew 18:21-32?

3. Describe the variety of deadly fruit produced from the root of bitterness. (*See* Ephesians 4:31 and Hebrews 12:15.)

PRACTICAL APPLICATION

But be ye doers of the word, and not hearers only, deceiving your own selves.
— James 1:22

1. What life disciplines and spiritual habits do you practice — or need to practice — to cultivate behavior the Bible defines as *kindness* and *tenderheartedness*? Are you equally gracious toward your colleagues, strangers, and your family, or are there inconsistencies in your conversation that demeans some while showing kindness to others? Examine your heart to determine and extract that root.

2. This lesson discusses the importance of intentionally putting away derogatory speech. Have you discovered and deliberately eliminated

any form of communication that grieves the Holy Spirit in your own life?

3. Do you recall a time that you failed to partner with the grace of God in dealing with bitterness? How did God give you another opportunity to embrace His grace so you could grace others?

TOPIC

The Tongue, a Releaser of Strife

SCRIPTURES

1. **Proverbs 10:19** — In the multitude of words there wanteth not sin: but he that refraineth his lips is wise.

2. **Proverbs 21:23** — Whoso keepeth his mouth and his tongue keepeth his soul from troubles.

3. **Ecclesiastes 3:7** — ...A time to keep silence, and a time to speak.

4. **James 3:2** — For in many things we offend all. If any man offend not in word, the same is a perfect man, and able also to bridle the whole body.

5. **James 3:3** — Behold, we put bits in the horses' mouths, that they may obey us; and we turn about their whole body.

6. **James 3:4** — Behold also the ships, which though they be so great, and are driven of fierce winds, yet are they turned about with a very small helm, whithersoever the governor listeth.

7. **James 3:5** — Even so the tongue is a little member, and boasteth great things. Behold, how great a matter a little fire kindleth!

8. **James 3:6** — And the tongue is a fire, a world of iniquity: so is the tongue among our members, that it defileth the whole body, and setteth on fire the course of nature; and it is set on fire of hell.

9. **James 3:7** — For every kind of beasts, and of birds, and of serpents, and of things in the sea, is tamed, and hath been tamed of mankind.

10. **James 3:8** — But the tongue can no man tame; it is an unruly evil, full of deadly poison.

11. **James 3:9** — Therewith bless we God, even the Father; and therewith curse we men, which are made after the similitude of God.

12. **James 3:10-13** — Out of the same mouth proceedeth blessing and cursing. My brethren, these things ought not so to be. Doth a fountain send forth at the same place sweet water and bitter? Can the fig tree, my brethren, bear olive berries? either a vine, figs? so can no fountain both yield salt water and fresh. Who is a wise man and endued with knowledge among you? let him shew out of a good conversation his works with meekness of wisdom.

GREEK WORDS

1. "offend" — πταίω (*ptaio*): to stumble; to err; to mess up

2. "in word" — ἐν λόγῳ (*en logo*): in what he says or speaks

3. "perfect" — τέλειος (*teleios*): a full-grown adult; pictures the process of transitioning from being youthful and immature to an individual who is full-grown and mature; in the New Testament it denotes spiritually mature individuals

4. "able" — δυνατός (*dunatos*): from δύναμις (*dunamis*), which is power or ability; depicts the assembled forces of an army whose combined strength enabled them to achieve unrivaled victories; these troops were so strong that they could not be resisted; δυνατός (*dunatos*): to have ability, power, or strength; to be able

5. "bridle" [the whole body] — χαλιναγωγέω (*chalinagogeo*): to bridle; to hold in check; to restrain; to control

6. "bits" — χαλινός (*chalinos*): a bridle; a bit

7. "obey" — πείθω (*peitho*): to sway from one direction to go in a different direction

8. "turn about" — μετάγω (*metago*): to lead differently; to turn about; to change direction

9. "behold" — ἰδού (*idou*): bewilderment, shock, amazement, and wonder

10. "great" — τηλικοῦτος (*telikoutos*): great in size; huge; vast; powerful in both size and ability

11. "turned about" — μετάγω (*metago*): to lead differently; to turn about; to change direction

12. "small helm" — ἐλαχίστου πηδαλίου (*elaxhistou pedaliou*): an extremely small rudder

13. "whithersoever the governor listeth" — ὅπου ἡ ὁρμὴ τοῦ εὐθύνοντος βούλεται (*hopou he horme tou euthunontos bouletai*): wherever the impulse of the one steering resolves to go; meaning the ship is directed by the one controlling the rudder

14. "even so" — Οὕτως καὶ (*houtos kai*): in the very same way

15. "the tongue" — ἡ γλῶσσα (*he glossa*): with a definite article, THE tongue

16. "little" — μικρός (*mikros*): very little; tiny; where we get the word micro or microscopic

17. "member" — μέλος (*melos*): member; organ of the body; used in antiquity to depict part of a ship needed to move the ship along; also used to depict weapons of war

18. "boasteth great things" — μεγάλα αὐχεῖ (*megala auchei*): to make a big commotion or noise

19. "little fire" — ἡλίκον πῦρ (*hekilon pur*): a small fire; a small blaze

20. "the tongue is a fire" — ἡ γλῶσσα πῦρ (*he glossa pur*): with a definite article, THE tongue is fire

21. "a world of iniquity" — ὁ κόσμος τῆς ἀδικίας (*ho kosmos tes adikias*): a universe or its own world, filled with hurt, injustice, wickedness, and violations

22. "defileth" — σπῖλος (*spilos*): to stain, defile, or to contaminate; to spill something that creates a stain; permanent; defilement; permanent contamination

23. "setteth on fire" — φλογίζω (*ploutidzo*): ignite; actual fire or raging passions

24. "and it is set on fire of hell" — καὶ φλογιζομένη ὑπὸ τῆς γεέννης (*kai ploudigomene hupo tes geennes*): being ignited and inflamed by hell itself

25. "beasts" — θηρίον (*therion*): wild beasts, dangerous animals, vicious killers; naturally wild beasts that are difficult to tame

26. "birds" — πετεινόν (*peteinon*): fowl; birds of all types

27. "serpents" — ἑρπετόν (*herpeton*): reptiles; snakes; crocodiles; all creeping reptiles

28. "things in the sea" — ἐνάλιος (*enalios*): all types of marine creatures

29. "tamed" — δαμάζω (*damadzo*): to domesticate, to subdue, or to bring under control; used to describe animal trainers who were experts at capturing and domesticating the wildest and most ferocious of beasts, such as lions, tigers, and bears; normally these animals would maul or

kill a person, but skilled trainers were able to take the wildest animals and domesticate them

30. "but" — δὲ (*de*): but; however; categorically; emphatically

31. "no man" — οὐδεὶς (*oudeis*): absolutely no one

32. "tame" — δαμάζω (*damadzo*): to domesticate, to subdue, or to bring under control; used to describe animal trainers who were experts at capturing and domesticating the wildest and most ferocious of beasts, such as lions, tigers, and bears; normally these animals would maul or kill a person, but skilled trainers were able to take the wildest animals and domesticate them

33. "unruly" — ἀκατάστατος (*akatastatos*): unstable; the idea of anarchy

34. "evil" — κακός (*kakos*): malice; spite; depicts words or actions that are bad or inappropriate

35. "full" — μεστός (*mestos*): full; fully loaded

36. "deadly poison" — ἰοῦ θανατηφόρου (*iou thanatephorou*): from ἰός (*ios*), poison that kills; rust that ruins, thus something that is ruinous; the word ἰός (*ios*) described the poison of asps; pictures words that injures others; also the word θανατηφόρος (*thanatephoros*), which means death producing; used by Greek writers to depict arrows or words that carried death

SYNOPSIS

In the Winter Palace in Saint Petersburg, Russia, there was a staircase which was once called Her Royal Majesty's Staircase. But eventually the name was changed to the October Staircase because on October 25, 1917, revolutionaries gained access through the entrance which was once used by various queens of Russia. Through a simple diversionary tactic — shots fired at the palace from the Peter and Paul Fortress on the other side of the Neva River — guards moved their attention from the entrance to the other side of the palace, leaving the entrance with absolutely no guards to protect the private quarters of the Romanov family.

They wandered through various rooms, eventually moving all the way down the hall into the White Dining Room where the provisional government was meeting. The revolutionaries arrested the provisional officials and sent them to prison at the Peter and Paul Fortress. This bitter coup initiated the Russian Civil War, which took the lives of millions of people.

The Bible tells us clearly that strife and bitterness are door openers that invite bitterness and every evil work to run rampant and destroy. You can overcome strife to prevent widespread destruction in your relationships with family and friends. First, you must realize the devil will incite distractions so he can find unprotected access. For this reason, it is important for you to guard your heart, guard your mind, guard your life, and guard your relationships against the devilish intruder of strife. Second, you must set a guard over your mouth so the devil cannot provoke corrupt communication to ensnare you with your own words.

The emphasis of this lesson:

In this lesson, we will examine how to recognize distractions to make sure your life remains protected on all fronts. If you can identify those points, then you can close those doors and the enemy will not find access to you through your emotions in order to trigger your tongue to release strife into your relationships.

Proverbs 10:19 tells us, "In the multitude of words there wanteth not sin: but he that refraineth his lips is wise." A paraphrase would be, "Where there's a lot of talk, there's a lot of sin, but when you learn how to control your mouth, you're smart." And Proverbs 21:23 says, "Whoso keepeth his mouth and his tongue keepeth his soul from troubles."

These two verses remind us that if your tongue is uncontrolled and you just say any and everything that comes to mind, you are going to get into trouble. But if you learn how to discipline your mouth and to keep your tongue in check, you will avoid unnecessary problems and prevent a lot of strife in life.

Ecclesiastes 3:7 wisely tells us there is "A time to rend, and a time to sew; a time to keep silence, and a time to speak." That lets us know that it's not always the right time to say certain things. Sometimes it's wiser to remain quiet. And that's what we see in James 3:2, "For in many things we offend all. If any man offend not in word, the same is a perfect man, and able also to bridle the whole body."

What Defines a 'Perfect Man'?

Notice that James used the word "offend" twice. He said, "For in many things we *offend* all. If any man *offends* not in word...." In both cases, this word "offend," the Greek word *ptaio*, means *to stumble*, or *to err*, or simply, *to mess up.* He literally is saying in many things we all mess up, but if any man does not mess up in word — and when it says, "in word," the Greek words *en logo*, it means *in speech* or *in what he says* — that man is a perfect man.

So how do you measure a perfect man? According to James 3:2, a perfect man is one who doesn't mess up in the things that he says. And this word "perfect" is the Greek word *teleios*, and depicts *a full-grown adult*; one who is no longer a child, but has really reached adulthood. It pictures *the process of transitioning from being youthful and immature to being an individual who is full grown and mature.*

And in the New Testament, it depicts people that are spiritually mature individuals. So now James tells us when you learn how to control your mouth — by guarding the words you speak — you are really transitioning from being youthful and immature to becoming a mature Christian.

Real spiritual maturity is not measured by how we preach, and it's not measured by how we prophesy. Spiritual maturity is measured by *what we say* and *what we do not say*. If you are watchful over the things you say, then the Bible affirms in this verse that you're reaching a state of spiritual maturity.

In fact, James 3:2 concludes, "…If any man offend not in word, the same is a perfect man, a mature man and *able* also to *bridle the whole body*." The word "able" is the Greek word *dunatos*, which means *to have ability, power, and strength*. This is very important because it's from the Greek word *dunamis*, which *pictures the assembled forces of an army whose combined strength enables them to achieve an unrivaled victory*. This word usage tells us it takes the strength of an army to control the tongue.

If you've learned to control your tongue, you have really attained something! It takes real strength and real maturity to tame the tongue. In fact, the Bible says if you can handle your mouth then you can "bridle the whole body." The word "bridle," the Greek word *chalinagogeo*, means *to hold in check; to control;* or *to restrain*. If you can control your tongue, then you can control anything in your body or in your life.

In the verses that follow James 3:2, James used the word "behold," the Greek word *idou*, many times. The word *idou* pictures *shock, amazement, bewilderment, and wonder*. It's as though James was saying, "Wow, this is amazing." Then he gave us an illustration. "Behold, we put bits in the horses' mouths, that they may obey us; and we turn about their whole body" (James 3:3). A *bit* is very, very small compared to the immense size of a muscular, powerful horse. But the Bible says when you put that bit into a horse's mouth it will obey.

James 3:3 continues, "Behold, we put bits in the horses' mouths, that they may *obey* us...." The word "obey" is a translation of the Greek word *pathos* which means you can even sway a horse *from going one direction and turn it around to go in a completely different direction*. The result of the horse's obedience is, "...And we turn about their whole body." The words "turn about" in Greek is the word *metago*, and it means *to lead differently; to turn about; to change directions*. Isn't it amazing that something as small as a little bit in a horse's mouth has the ability to completely control a horse and make it go in a different direction!

Our lesson on controlling our tongue continues in James 3:4: "Behold also the ships, which though they be so great, and are driven of fierce winds, yet are they *turned about* with a very *small helm*, whithersoever the governor listeth." Again we see the words "turned about," which means *to change direction*. But this time the change of direction is cause by "a very small helm," which describes *an extremely small rudder*. Just like a muscular, powerful horse can be turned around and controlled by a small bit in its mouth, these gargantuan ships can be controlled by a tiny little rudder. That really is amazing! No wonder James used the word "Behold" to describe the outcome.

And then he adds an important detail: "...Whithersoever the governor listeth." The Greek literally means *wherever the impulse of the one steering wants it to go*. The ship is directed by the one controlling the rudder. Whoever controls the rudder can determine the direction of that massive ship, even in the strongest of winds.

"Even so the tongue is a little member, and boasteth great things. Behold, how great a matter a little fire kindleth!" (James 3:5). In Greek, there is a definite article: *The* tongue. It means now James is really getting to his subject. He has used the illustration of a bit in a horse's mouth, and he's used the illustration of the rudder of a ship. Now he says let's get to the real subject — the tongue.

In the same way, the "tongue is a *little member*." The word "little" is the Greek word *mikros*, and it means *very little, tiny* — it's where we get the word micro and microscopic. And the word "member" is the Greek word *melos*, which describes *a member or an organ of the body*. But *melos* is also the very word used in ancient antiquity to depict parts of a ship needed to keep the ship moving along. Likewise, the tongue is necessary to keep society moving forward, but this word "member" — the Greek word *melos* — was also the very word used to depict weapons of war. It's so important to realize this means that the tongue can create progress, or the tongue can create war.

This verse continues by saying that this little member — the tongue — "boasteth great things." What does that mean? In Greek, it simply means *it makes a big commotion and makes a big noise*. And then, once again, he added the word "behold," the Greek word *idou*, which means *bewilderment, shock, amazement, and wonder*. "Isn't it amazing, shocking, and bewildering," James pointed out, "...the capability of the tongue to kindle a flame." It is astounding the damage that can be done by the fires that are started by such a small member of our bodies — the tongue.

James 3:6 then says, "And the tongue is a fire, *a world of iniquity*: so is the tongue among our members, that it defileth the whole body, and setteth on fire the course of nature; and it is set on fire of hell." Here, James said the tongue is "a world of iniquity." The Greek literally says *ho kosmos tes adikias*. The Greek word *kosmos* is the word for *the universe; its own world*, and *adikias* describes *injury, violations, or injustice*. In this verse, James said that the tongue *is a universe of its own filled with hurt, injustice, wickedness, and all kinds of violations*. That is the capability of the tongue that is not controlled.

But James 3:6 continues: "And the tongue is a fire, a world of iniquity: so is the tongue among our members, that it *defileth* the whole body...." The word "defiles" is the Greek word *spilos*, and it denotes *to stain, to defile*, or *to contaminate*. It means *to spill something that creates a stain; a permanent defilement*, or *a permanent contamination*. Think how many people's lives have been stained because of what someone said. That's exactly what James is telling us. The tongue can defile the whole body "and *setteth on fire* the course of nature." "Sets on fire," from the Greek word *ploutidzo*, means *ignited* and it can refer to *an actual fire* or *raging passions* that are out of control. The Greek literally means it is *ignited and inflamed by hell itself*.

James then gave us a few examples of things that can be tamed: "For every kind of beasts, and of birds, and of serpents, and of things in the sea, is tamed, and hath been tamed of mankind" (James 3:7). First, he mentioned "beasts" which is the Greek word *therion*. This word *therion* — translated as "beasts" — describes *four-footed wild beasts, dangerous animals,* and *vicious killers.* These beasts are *naturally wild beasts that are nearly impossible to tame.* Next on the list is "birds," the Greek word *peteinon,* which refers to *any fowl of the air, birds of all types,* like parrots. Even parrots can be tamed and taught to speak.

The list of tamable creatures in James 3:7 continues with "serpents." The word "serpents," the Greek word *herpeton,* describes *reptiles, snakes, and crocodiles; all creeping, crawling things.* On the program, Rick expressed his amazement that these creatures made the list of "tamable" things. When he was a young man growing up, he owned snakes, and he readily admitted that snakes are nearly impossible to tame. In fact, *all* these creatures James mentioned in this passage are nearly impossible to tame.

Though wild, they can be tamed. Birds of the air can be taught to speak, and reptiles, according to this verse, can also be tamed. And then James mentioned "things in the sea," which in Greek, refers to *all types of marine creatures.* If you've ever gone to a marine show, you've seen whales jumping through hoops. So, even marine animals can be tamed. The Bible says that all these creatures are *"tamed,* and hath been *tamed* of mankind." The Greek word *damadzo,* translated "tamed," means *to domesticate, to subdue, and to bring under control.* It was the very word used *to describe animal trainers who were experts at capturing and domesticating the wildest and most ferocious of beasts, such as lions, tigers, and bears.* Although these animals would normally maul or kill a person, skilled trainers were able to take the wildest animals and domesticate them. And according to this verse, all these creatures can be subdued, and they can be domesticated.

But then James said, "But…." *"But the tongue* can no man tame; it is an unruly evil, full of deadly poison" (James 3:8). In Greek, the word translated as "but," means *categorically* and *emphatically.* And again we see the definite article, meaning *the* tongue. James continued, "But the tongue can *no man* tame…." "No man" in Greek is *oudeis,* and it means that *absolutely no one* can tame the tongue. And the word "tame" is again the Greek word *damadzo,* the word we just learned that means *to domesticate, to subdue, or to bring under control.* So, James said the tongue cannot be domesticated — it can't be subdued. And furthermore, James said the tongue "…is an *unruly* evil, full of deadly poison." The word "unruly" is the Greek word *akatastatos,* which means *unstable* and carries the idea of *anarchy.* James made it clear — the tongue is unstable and filled with anarchy, and it cannot be tamed.

To say the tongue is an "unruly evil" is to describe its capability of releasing words filled with *malice or spite*, or *words that are bad or inappropriate*. James also said the tongue is "full of deadly poison." The word "full," the Greek word *mestos*, means *fully loaded; loaded to the maximum*. And it is fully loaded with "deadly poison" — translated from the Greek words *ios thanatephorou*. The word *ios*, translated as "deadly," denotes *poison that kills*, or *rust that ruins, thus it is something ruinous*. It describes *the poison of asps and deadly serpents*, and it also *pictures words that injure others*. The Greek word *thanatephorou*, translated "poison," means *death producing*. It was used by Greek writers to depict arrows or words that carried death.

And this deadly poison is what is in the tongue if the tongue is not brought under control. It's like an asp that is filled with deadly poison just waiting for the moment to sink its fangs into a victim and inject the venom. That's what the Bible says about the tongue.

James 3:9 remarkably says, "Therewith bless we God, even the Father; and therewith curse we men, which are made after the similitude of God." Both blessing and cursing are released by the tongue. The word "bless" is the Greek word *eulogeo*, which means *to say something good*. The word "curse" means *to speak words that bring others down*.

James concluded, "Out of the same mouth proceeds blessing and cursing. My brethren, these things ought not so to be. Doth a fountain send forth at the same place sweet water and bitter? Can the fig tree, my brethren, bear olive berries? Either a vine, figs? So can no fountain both yield salt water and fresh? Who is a wise man and endued with knowledge among you? Let him shew out of a good conversation his works with meekness of wisdom" (James 3:10-13).

If you think you're spiritually mature, then this is what you should demonstrate with your life and through your words. The Bible defines good conversation as polite, appropriate speech. This is the exact opposite of corrupt communication. The tongue releases strife into the earth. The tongue can benefit society and cause it to advance, or the tongue can create and provoke divisiveness and war. What types of words are released by *your* tongue? Life and death are in the power of the tongue. If you will control your tongue you will deliver yourself from trouble in life.

In our next lesson, we will continue to study *how* to tame the tongue and quench the fires of devilish incitement.

STUDY QUESTIONS

Study to shew thyself approved unto God, a workman that needeth not to be ashamed, rightly dividing the word of truth.
— 2 Timothy 2:15

1. If you can control your tongue and the words you speak, you can bring order and alignment to your body, your thoughts, and your attitudes. In your own words, what is the true measurement of spiritual maturity according to James 3:10-13?

2. No "man" can tame the tongue, but the power of the Holy Spirit can. In John 14:26 (*AMPC*), Jesus said, "But the Comforter (Counselor, Helper, Intercessor, Advocate, Strengthener, Standby), the Holy Spirit, Whom the Father will send in My name [in My place, to represent Me and act on My behalf], He will teach you all things...." Consider the ministry of the Holy Spirit and how you can rely upon His help and guidance to tame your tongue.

3. In this lesson, what did you learn about the vast capability of the tongue — a universe of its own, a world of iniquity?

PRACTICAL APPLICATION

But be ye doers of the word, and not hearers only,
deceiving your own selves.
— James 1:22

1. According to James 3:6 (*NKJV*), the tongue "is a fire, a world of iniquity...and it is set on fire by hell." Once spoken, words cannot be reclaimed. Since from the heart the mouth speaks (*see* Matthew 12:34), how do you monitor your thoughts to shield your heart against incitement and pollution?

2. A fountain cannot produce both fresh and salt water at the same time. Yet a person can speak contradictory — even opposite — words in almost the same breath. Is that quality evident in your life? If so, what measures will you take to change that practice? If not, what can you do to maintain purity and consistency in your conversation?

3. Malicious words of criticism, sarcasm, gossip, and ridicule are the vilest types of evil communication because they transmit the hatred and rebellion of Satan himself who inspires such words. Are you speaking or being influenced by this kind of talk? If so, take heed and make a change quickly — neither the hearer nor the speaker of malicious words will go unscathed.

LESSON 4

TOPIC

The Demonic Source of Strife

SCRIPTURES

1. **James 3:14** — But if ye have bitter envying and strife in your hearts, glory not, and lie not against the truth.
2. **James 3:15** — This wisdom descendeth not from above, but is earthly, sensual, devilish.
3. **James 3:16** — For where envying and strife is, there is confusion and every evil work.
4. **James 3:14** (*RIV*) — If you have an inner attitude so bitter that you are unkind, sour, sharp, sarcastic, scornful, cynical, mocking, contemptuous, and wounding of others; if you are driven to see your view or agenda adopted at the expense of others, even irritated, infuriated, irate, annoyed, provoked, fuming, or incensed with others and so filled with strife inside your heart that you are blinded to the desires or needs of others — and are jockeying for advantage even if it is to the disadvantage of others — you must stop these actions and attitudes that are being carried out at the expense of others and quit projecting yourself as doing it all with right motives, because it isn't true.
5. **James 3:15** (*RIV*) — This is emphatically not the wisdom that comes down from Heaven, but on the contrary, it emphatically is from a low-level earthly realm, it is pure soulish activity, and anyone who is thinking and behaving like this is clearly under the influence of demonic activity.
6. **James 3:16** (*RIV*) — For where people have bitter attitudes that make them unkind, sour, sharp, sarcastic, scornful, cynical, mocking, con-

temptuous, and wounding of others, and when they are driven to see their view or agenda adopted at the expense of others, and they are irritated, infuriated, irate, annoyed, provoked, fuming, incensed with others and so blinded to the desires or needs of others that they are jockeying for some kind of advantage of position even to the disadvantage of others, it results in anarchy and every stinking work.

7. **James 3:17** — But the wisdom that is from above is first pure, then peaceable, gentle, and easy to be intreated, full of mercy and good fruits, without partiality, and without hypocrisy.

8. **James 3:17** (*RIV*) — Wisdom that comes from a heavenly source is first of all recognizable because of its impeccable behavior. It comes with a dominating sense of peace and is characterized by a mild, kind, temperate, calm, and gentle behavior that comforts, calms, softens, and brings healing to others. Real heavenly wisdom gets along easily with others and never demands its own way with ugly and unreasonable behavior. It is filled to the brim with so much compassion that it finds a way to be helpful in any way possible. Such wisdom does not practice favoritism. It is authentic and genuine.

GREEK WORDS

1. "bitter" — πικρία (*pikria*): an inner bitterness or attitude toward someone, toward a group, or toward a situation; inner poison that causes one to eventually become unkind, sour, sharp, sarcastic, scornful, cynical, mocking, contemptuous, and wounding

2. "envying" — ζῆλος (*zelos*): a self-consumed person who is driven to see his agenda adopted; one who is competitive; denotes one upset because someone else achieved more or received more; one who is jealous, envious, resentful, and filled with ill will for the one who got what he wanted; irritated, infuriated, irate, annoyed, provoked, and fuming; one who is incensed

3. "strife" — ἐριθεία (*eritheia*): a political party; often translated "a party spirit" because of its connection to political systems and political parties; pictures individuals or groups of people who push their agenda and ideas, fighting fiercely to see their platform accepted; self-seeking ambition that is more concerned about itself and the fulfillment of its own wants, desires, and pleasures than it is in meeting the needs in others; pictures one so bent on getting what he wants that he is willing to do anything, say anything, and sacrifice any standard, rules,

or relationship to achieve his goals; a selfish, self-focused attitude that is engrossed with its own desires and ambitions; one so self-consumed that he is blinded to the desires or ambitions of others; pictures a person who is jockeying for some kind of position

4. "in your hearts" — ἐν τῇ καρδίᾳ ὑμῶν (*n te kardia humon*): literally, in your hearts; indicating this is a heart issue

5. "glory" — κατακαυχάομαι (*katakauchaomai*): over-exalting at the expense of another; actions that exalt one and downgrade another

6. "lie" — ψεύδομαι (*pseudomai*): one who walks in a pretense that is untrue; who intentionally misrepresents facts or truths

7. "descendeth" — κατέρχομαι (*katerchomai*): literally, does not come down; descend

8. "from above" — ἄνωθεν (*anothen*): from above; meaning, from a heavenly source

9. "earthly" — ἐπίγειος (*epigeios*): from the earth; right from the earth; referring to the earth realm

10. "sensual" — υχικός (*psuchikos*): soulish; belonging to the soulish realm

11. "devilish" — αιμονιώδης (*daimoniodes*): demonic; demon-like; influenced by demons

12. "confusion" — ἀκαταστασία (*akatastasia*): anarchy, chaos, insubordination, or some kind of attitude or action that creates upheaval, unrest, or instability; the attitude or actions of a person who creates some type of disastrous disturbance; any lack of stability, confusion, or anything unstable

13. "evil" — φαῦλος (*phaulos*): something that stinks; something that is rotting, such as meat full of maggots; dead, decaying, and stinking

14. "from above" — ἄνωθεν (*anothen*): from above; meaning, from a heavenly source

15. "first" — πρῶτον (*proton*): first and foremost

16. "pure" — ἁγνός (*hagnos*): pure inside and out; uncontaminated

17. "peaceable" — εἰρηνικός (*eirenikos*): peace-conquering; peace-dominating

18. "gentle" — ἐπιεικής (*epieikes*): mild; gentle

19. "easy to be entreated" — εὐπειθής (*eupeithes*): pictures one that is reasonable or agreeable, as opposed to one who is ugly and obstinate in his behavior

20. "without hypocrisy" — ἀνυπόκριτος (*anupokritos*): authentic, genuine; it is the opposite of something pretended, simulated, faked, feigned, or phony; one who is authentic

SYNOPSIS

In the previous lessons, we noted that on October 25, 1917, guards prevented revolutionaries from penetrating the main gate of the Winter Palace of Saint Petersburg, Russia. Insurgents then began bombing from the other side of the palace against the façade as a diversionary tactic. That tactic was effective. When all the guards inside relocated to the other side of the palace to defend it against the bombing, the other side they had been protecting was suddenly open for access. Around 2:00 a.m., revolutionaries entered the palace through the area previously called Her Royal Majesty's Staircase. That night, however, it became known as the legendary October Staircase where revolutionaries entered to occupy the palace.

As the revolutionaries ascended the stairs, immediately they entered the White Hall. They must have been stunned by the grandeur of the rooms they saw inside the palace. Then they began to wander into various private rooms. They wandered into the Gold Room — a room adorned with 11 pounds of gold. From there, they wandered into the Boudoir, then the Music Room, and finally down the long tapestry hallway that eventually led them into the magnificent Malachite Room.

Attached to the Malachite Room was the White Dining Room where 17 members of the provisional government were meeting that night. They actually had begun their meeting in the Malachite Room, but when the bombing began, they left the Malachite Room and moved into the attached White Dining Room. That's where they were sitting and meeting when the revolutionaries entered and arrested them. That very night, they were sent to the Peter and Paul Fortress where they were imprisoned, as the Russian Civil War was launched in full force.

Bitterness, envy, and strife at work in politics is so ugly. When you see those qualities operating in relationships it can be devastating.

The emphasis of this lesson:

Strife is a killer of nations and of relationships. But you can keep its destructive bitterness out of your life. If you'll listen to the Holy Spirit and obey the Scriptures, you can guard yourself on every front and avoid

a lot of trouble. There is a demonic source to strife. And if you don't close the door to strife, all kinds of trouble will come through that door into your life, into your mind, into your emotions, and into your relationships.

Bitterness, Envy and Strife — A Heart Issue!

When people are embroiled in a moment of anger, they'll make statements like, "I just have to say this…." Then, they'll proceed to say something they will usually regret. Saying everything you feel is not always wise. In fact, we're told in Proverbs that if we'll control our tongue, we will keep ourselves from a lot of trouble (*see* Proverbs 21:23). And Ecclesiastes 3:7 tells us there's a time to be silent, and there's a time to speak. And when you're upset, that is not always the right moment to speak — especially when strife has its origin in demonic activity.

James 3:14 says, "If ye have *bitter envying* and *strife* in your hearts, glory not, and lie not against the truth." Let's dissect this verse because it's loaded with revelation. The word "bitter" is the Greek word *pikria*, and it's a terrible word. *Pikria* denotes *an inner bitterness or attitude toward someone or toward a group or toward a situation*. It is an inner poison that causes one to eventually become unkind, sour, sharp, sarcastic, scornful, cynical, mocking, contemptuous, and even wounding.

The word "envy" is a translation of the Greek word *zealous*, which depicts *a person who is so driven to see his own agenda adopted that he's become competitive*. It denotes one who is upset because someone else has achieved or received more than him. It depicts one who is jealous, envious, resentful, and filled with ill-will; one who is irritated, infuriated, irate, annoyed, provoked, and fuming, or one who is incensed. These are really strong words!

The word "strife" is the Greek word *eritheia*. The word *eritheia* was the old Greek word to describe *a political party or "a party spirit."* We see it used like this in First Corinthians 1, where we read about strife and division operating in the church at Corinth. The word *eritheia* also described the church being divided and filled with strife. The church at Corinth had divided into different parties, different groups, and now they were fighting each other, and all of this was happening right inside the church.

But this word "strife," the Greek word *eritheia*, describes a political party, or it is often translated as a "party spirit" because of its connection to political systems and political parties. It *pictures individuals or groups of people who push their agenda and ideas, fighting fiercely to see their platform accepted.* It depicts *self-seeking ambition that is more concerned about itself and the fulfillment of its own wants, desires, and pleasures than it is in meeting the needs of others.*

The word "strife" also *pictures one so bent on getting what he wants that he's willing to do anything or say anything* — including the release of strife. This person is willing *to sacrifice any standard, rule, or relationship to achieve his objective.* It pictures a selfish, self-focused attitude that is engrossed with one's own desires and ambitions. A person filled with strife is so self-consumed that he is blinded to the needs and desires of others, or it even pictures a person that is jockeying for some kind of position. And what's really interesting is James said that envy and strife are "in your *hearts,*" which indicates this is a heart issue.

Sometimes people say, "I've just got to say what's on my mind," or "I've got to get this off my chest." We've already seen in our previous lesson that the tongue releases the fires of hell (*see* James 3:6). And if you have strife in your heart by all means keep your mouth shut, because out of the abundance of your heart, your mouth will release disastrous effects.

James 3:14 continues, "…Glory not, and lie not against the truth." The word "glory" is translation from the Greek word *katakauchaomai,* which describes *over-exalting at the expense of another.* It depicts *actions that exalt one and downgrade another.* If you find that your tongue is wanting to exalt *yourself, your* position, and *your* own ideas by humiliating someone else, you are operating in a wrong spirit.

Verse 14 concludes, "…And *lie* not against the truth." The word "lie" is the Greek word *pseudomai,* and it pictures *a person who walks under pretense that is untrue,* or *one who intentionally misrepresents facts or truths.* Usually people who are feeling this way will say, "I just believe that I'm right," and then begin to slaughter the other person with their words of untruth. But James tells us not to lie against the truth, and nothing about defending an untruth is right.

And James 3:15 gives us the reason we are not to "lie against the truth": "This wisdom *descendeth* not from above, but is earthly, sensual, devilish." The word "descendeth," or descend, is the Greek word *katerchomai,* and in this usage it actually means *it does not come down.* And it doesn't come down from a heavenly source — it is earthly. The word "earthly" is the

Greek word *epigeios*. *Epigeios* is a compound word from *epi* meaning *upon*, and *geios* from the word *ge*, which means *the earth*.

When *epi* and *geios* are compounded to form *epigeios*, the meaning is that such wisdom is *from a low-level earthly realm*; it's *right from the earth*. There is nothing heavenly about the one whose attitudes or behavior reflect such "wisdom." This is as earthly as it can be. But then James added the word "sensual." The word "sensual" — the Greek word *psuchikos* — means *soulish* or *belonging to the soulish realm*. Notice, this is not spiritual activity. This is *soul* activity, which includes manipulation.

In addition to earthly and sensual — *originating from the earth and soulish* — James then added that this so-called wisdom from lying against the truth is "devilish." The word "devilish" is a translation from the Greek word *daimoniodes*, which means it is *demonic, demon-like,* or *influenced by demons*. This word — *daimoniodes* — is normally translated *demonized*. It depicts *a person whose mind or emotions have come under the influence of demon spirits.* So, when you put it all together, James is actually telling his readers when a person walks in bitter envying and strife, his behavior is an obvious indication that his soul has come under the influence of demonic activity. We know this is *not* heavenly behavior because James 3:16 tells us, "For where envying and strife is, there is confusion and every evil work."

The word translated "envying" is the Greek word *zelos*, which depicts *a self-consumed person who is driven to see his agenda adopted.* This person is *competitive, jealous, envious, resentful,* and filled with ill-will for the one who got what he wanted or becomes upset because someone else has achieved more or received more than him. It depicts *a person that is irritated, infuriated, irate, annoyed, provoked, and fuming or even incensed.* What a profound picture of the word *envy.*

And the word "strife" in this verse is the same Greek word *eritheia* that we saw in James 3:14. Again, *eritheia* depicts a *"party spirit."* In other words, such a person is engrossed in pushing his own agenda, ideas, and desires. An individual with a "party spirit" will do everything possible to fight and ensure that his agenda is implemented. This person is so self-absorbed and consumed by himself and his own selfish goals that he's blinded to the desires or even the needs of others. All he cares about is jockeying to secure some kind of win or position.

James made it very clear: "For where envying and strife is, there is *con-fusion* and every *evil* work." The word "confusion" is the Greek word for *anarchy*, and its effects are *upheaval*, *unrest*, and *instability*. Consider the seriousness of these heart attitudes: Envy and strife release *anarchy*, *chaos*, and its destructiveness into homes, into churches, into nations, and into relationships.

This word "confusion" is the same Greek word that was used to *describe plants with thorns*. When you get near them, you're going to be cut or hurt. By using this particular word, James is saying you can become entrapped in thorny conversations that produce anarchy in you and in your relationships. James concludes that not only does envy and strife cause confusion, but it also produces "every evil work." The word "evil" is the Greek word *phaulos*, and it describes *something that stinks* or *something rotting*. It pictures rotting meat full of maggots.

Consider the *Renner Interpretive Version* of James 3:14-16:

> If you have an inner attitude so bitter that you are unkind, sour, sharp, sarcastic, scornful, cynical, mocking, contemptuous, and wounding of others; if you're driven to see your view or agenda adopted at the expense of others, even being irritated, infuriated, irate, annoyed, provoked, fuming or incensed with others and so filled with strife inside your heart that you're blinded to the desires or needs of others — and are jockeying for advantage even if it is to the disadvantage of others — you must stop these actions and attitudes that are being carried out at the expense of others and quit projecting yourself as doing it all with right motives, because it isn't true.

> This is emphatically not the wisdom that comes down from Heaven, but on the contrary, it emphatically is from a low-level earthly realm, it is pure soulish activity, and anyone who is thinking and behaving like this is clearly under the influence of demonic activity.

> For where people have bitter attitudes that make them unkind, sour, sharp, sarcastic, scornful, cynical, mocking, contemptuous, and wounding of others, and when they are driven to see their view or agenda adopted at the expense of others, and they are irritated, infuriated, irate, annoyed, provoked, fuming, incensed with others and so blinded to the desires or needs of others that they're jockeying for some kind of advantage or

position even to the disadvantage of others, it results in anarchy and every stinking work.

But then we come to verse 17, and James continued: "But the wisdom that is from above is first pure, then peaceable, gentle, and easy to be intreated, full of mercy and good fruits, without partiality, and without hypocrisy" (James 3:17). Notice what James said: "...the wisdom that comes *from above*...." THIS wisdom "from above," is the Greek word *anothen*, which means *from a heavenly source*. It IS *from above,* as opposed to earthly wisdom, which is a lower level, from-the-earth wisdom.

And this heavenly wisdom from above is "first pure." The word "first" in Greek is the word *proton*, and it means *first and foremost*. The word "pure" — the Greek word *hagnos* — describes something that is *pure inside and out, completely uncontaminated*. It denotes something that is impeccable in behavior as opposed to something that is unruly. So the first attribute of heavenly wisdom is first and foremost pure, inside and out, and completely uncontaminated.

James then described the wisdom from above as "peaceable." The word "peaceable" in Greek is the word *eirenikos*. It is a compound of the word *eirene,* which is the word for *peace,* and the Greek word *nikos*, which means *to conquer*. When you compound these two Greek words — *eirene* and *nikos* — it means *to behave in a right spirit, projecting a peaceful, conquering attitude*. This is a dominating sense of peace as opposed to a strife-filled attitude that steals peace. James also described the wisdom from above as "gentle," the Greek word *epieikes*, which means just that — *gentle* and *mild*. It depicts one that is temperate and calm. It denotes one whose character comforts, calms, softens, or even brings healing as opposed to one who demands his way or is easily angered.

Continuing his attributes of true wisdom, James said that it is "easy to be entreated." "Easy to be entreated" pictures *one that is reasonable or agreeable*. When you're in a spirit of strife you're *not* reasonable and you're *not* agreeable. James also said that true wisdom is full of mercy and good fruits, and that this kind of wisdom is "without hypocrisy." In the Greek, to be "without hypocrisy" means to be *authentic, genuine* — this is the opposite of something pretended, simulated, feigned, faked or phony.

The *RIV* of James 3:17 is this:

Wisdom that comes from a heavenly source is first of all recognizable because of its impeccable behavior. It comes with a dominating sense of peace and is characterized by a mild, kind, temperate, calm, and gentle behavior that comforts, calms, softens and brings healing to others. Real heavenly wisdom gets along easily with others and never demands its own way with ugly and unreasonable behavior. It is filled to the brim with so much compassion that it finds a way to be helpful in any way possible. Such wisdom does not practice favoritism. It is authentic and genuine.

This is quite a comparison. Devilish operations come from a low-level earthly realm to cause hurt, versus the healing and peace that come from a heavenly realm. It is amazing. Even if you're in a moment where you are disagreeing with someone, you don't have to surrender to those demonic forces that want to provoke a heated escalation until the disagreement becomes a battlefield.

You can yield to the wisdom that comes from above and allow the Holy Spirit to work in you to release healing into that situation. It's better for you to obey Proverbs 21:23 which instructs you to keep your tongue and deliver yourself from trouble. Allow the Holy Spirit to help you tame your tongue by acting on Ecclesiastes 3:7 — there is a time to speak, and there is a time to be quiet. If rage is erupting in your heart, that is *not* the time to speak. Calm down and let the Holy Spirit deal with you instead. Finally, when there's a sense of peace dominating in your heart then you can return to the conversation and your words will be beneficial. Remember: *You can* and *you must* close the door to strife. Do not surrender to strife because strife — with all its evil works — has its origin in the demonic realm. And you, my friend, can operate in the heavenly realm.

STUDY QUESTIONS

Study to shew thyself approved unto God, a workman that needeth not to be ashamed, rightly dividing the word of truth.
— 2 Timothy 2:15

1. When people jockey for an advantage in position, even to the disadvantage of others, it results in anarchy — in nations and in relationships. You've observed this ugly scenario in politics. It's even more tragic when it takes place within a marriage, a ministry, or a family.

Study Romans 12:10 and First Corinthians 12 (*AMPC*) to discover the true antidote to this dangerous behavior.

2. Study and contrast "the wisdom from below" and "the wisdom from above" as outlined in James 3:15-17. (The Greek word *eritheia*, describes a political party or it is often translated as a "party spirit" because of its connection to political systems and political parties. It pictures individuals or groups of people who push their agenda and ideas; fighting fiercely to see their platform accepted to the exclusion of others. This was the spirit at work in the take-over at the Winter Palace in 1917. It is the same spirit at work in governments around the world today.)

3. Review the *RIV* of James 3:17:

   Wisdom that comes from a heavenly source is first of all recognizable because of its impeccable behavior. It comes with a dominating sense of peace and is characterized by a mild, kind, temperate, calm, and gentle behavior that comforts, calms, softens, and brings healing to others. Real heavenly wisdom gets along easily with others and never demands its own way with ugly and unreasonable behavior. It is filled to the brim with so much compassion that it finds a way to be helpful in any way possible. Such wisdom does not practice favoritism. It is authentic and genuine.

PRACTICAL APPLICATION

But be ye doers of the word, and not hearers only,
deceiving your own selves.
—James 1:22

1. Devilish incitement is a strategic attack to provoke you to speak words that will harm others and hinder you. Have you allowed frustration to give place to demonic operations in your life?

2. The Bible says that wisdom from God is first pure, then peaceable, gentle, and easy to get along with — easy to be intreated, full of mercy and good fruits, without partiality, and without hypocrisy. Does this sound like a description of your personality? If not, what alterations do you need to make to align your ways with God's?

3. The gospel of James is very clear when it says that wherever there is envying and strife there is also confusion. The word "confusion" is

the Greek word for *anarchy*. Consider the seriousness of these heart attitudes: Envy and strife release anarchy and its destructiveness into homes, into churches, into nations, and into relationships. Hide the Word of God in your heart daily as a safeguard against the penetration of such treachery (*see* Psalm 119:11).

LESSON 5

TOPIC

How To Put an End to Strife

SCRIPTURES

1. **Hebrews 12:14** — Follow peace with all men, and holiness, without which no man shall see the Lord.
2. **Hebrews 12:15** — Looking diligently lest any man fail of the grace of God; lest any root of bitterness springing up trouble you, and thereby many be defiled.

GREEK WORDS

1. "follow" — **διώκω** (*dioko*): a hunting term: to follow; to chase; to pursue; to hunt
2. "peace" — **εἰρήνη** (*eirene*): the cessation of war; conflict put away; rebuilding; reconstruction; a time of peace
3. "holiness" — **ἅγιος** (*hagios*): holy, consecrated, different, separate
4. "looking diligently" — **ἐπίσκοπος** (*episkopos*): from **ἐπί** (*epi*) and **σκοπος** (*skopos*); the word **ἐπί** (*epi*) means over, and the word **σκοπος** (*skopos*) means to look; compounded, to look over, oversight, administrate, manage, a supervisory position, bishop
5. "fail" — **ὑστερέω** (*hustereo*): to fall short; to have a deficit; to run out
6. "grace" — **χάρις** (*charis*): an empowering touch that transforms
7. "root" — **ῥίζα** (*ridza*): something deeply rooted
8. "bitterness" — **πικρία** (*pikria*): an inward attitude that is so bitter, it produces a scowl on one's face
9. "springing up" — **φύω** (*phuo*): a small plant that pierces its way through the soil

10. "trouble" — ἐνοχλέω (*enochleo*): harassed, hounded, troubled
11. "defiled" — μιαίνω (*miaino*): stained, polluted; permanently affected

SYNOPSIS

In the previous lessons, we outlined the events of national strife, anarchy, and insurrection that started the Russian Civil War in 1917.

On the evening of October 25, at 9 p.m. at the site of the Winter Palace in Saint Petersburg, Russia, guards prevented revolutionaries from forcibly entering the palace. After using a diversionary tactic to provoke guards to leave one side of the palace unprotected, revolutionaries penetrated the palace and staged a coup at 2 a.m. on October 26.

Wandering through rooms and corridors of exquisite decor they made their way into the Malachite Room — a fabulous room whose exteriors are veneered with two tons of malachite. From there, the revolutionaries entered the relatively small White Dining Room where the provisional government was meeting.

The room had been used as the private dining quarters of the royal family. Its walls were surrounded with tapestries of different continents of the world. So as the Romanov family would have dinner they would be reminded of their immense power over vast parts of the world. But on that night, the 17 members of the provisional government seated around the table were arrested as that coup ensued.

In fact, for many years, the clock on the mantle of that room was stopped at exactly at 2:10 to commemorate the exact time when the provisional government was arrested and sent to prison across the river inside the Peter and Paul Fortress. It is amazing that such a revolutionary history-making moment began in such a small room.

Even today, when you go into the White Dining Room, the size of it is very unimpressive compared to the other rooms inside the Winter Palace. It's just a small room, but in that very small room events took place so demonic in origin they changed all of human history and affected millions of lives. The Russian Civil War was launched that night and lasted until 1922. Politics were changed all over the world because life-altering evil was unleashed in a small dining room that sprang up into wickedness that continued to rage across the planet.

The emphasis of this lesson:

Strife is a powerful, deadly influence. And the root of it is demonic. Strife and its consequences are destructive. In this lesson, we will study how to put an end to strife and shut the door to keep it out of your relationships for good.

Hebrews 12:14-15 says, "Follow peace with all men, and holiness, without which no man shall see the Lord: Looking diligently lest any man fail of the grace of God; lest any root of bitterness springing up trouble you, and thereby many be defiled."

Notice how the very first words of verse 14 say "Follow *peace*...." Let's begin with that word "peace." The word "peace" in Greek is the word *eirene,* and it describes *the cessation of war, a decision to put away the weapons and conflict.* The Greek word *eirene,* translated as "peace," actually describes a time of rebuilding and a time of reconstruction — a time of peace.

Pursue Peace — Hunt and Capture It!

The writer of Hebrews is telling us we have to make the decision to put the conflict away and begin a time of rebuilding. A cessation of war is a choice. And he informs us that we have to "follow peace" in order to obtain it. The word "follow" in Greek is the old Greek word *dioko,* and it can be translated *to follow.* But *dioko* was first *a hunting term* that pictured a hunter who picked up all his hunting gear, dressed in his camouflage clothing, and pursued an animal until he finally got his game.

This is a picture of a hunter who is so committed to get his game, that the hunter is going to *dioko* — follow and follow and follow and not stop — until he gets what he's after. He's going to follow the tracks of the animal. He's going to chase the scent of the animal. The hunter will look for every little broken twig along the way to see where the animal has been.

He's going to follow, and not stop following, until finally he captures his game. That's the meaning of the word — *dioko* — that is used here. This means, if we want to have peace in our relationships, if we want to have the cessation of war in our family, put all the weapons aside. Enter into a time of reconstruction and rebuilding and a time of peace because we can't wait for peace to come to us. We have to make a decision and say: *I'm going to put on my hunting clothes. I'm going to follow the tracks of peace. I'm going to do whatever I have to do to obtain peace in my relationships, and I'm not going to stop until I have it.* You cannot wait for peace to come to you; you must take the initiative to go after it.

But we're not just to pursue peace with those in our household; the verse goes on to say, "Follow peace *with all men....*" It's God's will for us to have peace in our relationships with everyone. Hebrews 12:14 continues, "...and *holiness*, without which no man shall see the Lord." The word "holiness" is a form of the Greek word *hagios* — translated here as "holiness" — and it describes something that is *holy, consecrated, separate*, or something that is *different*. God is calling us to a higher standard — one that is holy, consecrated, separated, and different.

People in the world can slug it out, and they can verbally fight it out, but God has called us to "holiness," the Greek word *hagios*. God has called us to a higher standard — to act differently. It doesn't matter what everybody else is doing, it only matters what God is asking of us. And God has asked us not to behave like others, but to come to a higher level — to be separate; to be different; to follow after peace; to be holy.

Hebrews 12:14 concludes, "Follow peace with all men, and holiness, *without which no man shall see the Lord.*" This begs the question: Does this mean that if you have bitterness in your heart or a lack of peace you're not going to go to heaven? No, it doesn't mean that. There are a lot of people who die with bitterness, but they went to heaven. Then what *does* this mean?

When the Bible says, "without which no man shall see the Lord," the actual Greek words mean, *will not be admitted into the immediate presence of the Lord.* In other words, strife is a blocker. Strife will block you from the presence of the Lord. If you have strife working in your heart, you can be in a church service where everyone else is experiencing the presence of God, but you'll feel nothing because strife is a blocker. It blocks you from the anointing; it blocks you from the presence of the Lord.

If you do have strife in your life, you must become determined to be rid of it. The first step is to make the decision to be strife free and committed to a life filled with peace. You could start by making a confession to yourself like the following:

"I'm going to obtain peace in my relationships. If I have to follow after it, follow after it, and follow after it some more, *I will not stop* until, finally, I capture peace with _____ (my spouse; my children; my siblings; my friends, etc.). I'm going to put on my hunting clothes, and I'm going to capture peace. I'm determined; I'm not going to stop until I finally have peace with *all* men. I'm going to behave differently. I'm going to come up to the standard that God expects of me, and, as a result, I'm going to experience the presence of God."

But this is not a casual hunting trip. To obtain peace — and maintain it — takes serious commitment. That's why it says in Hebrews 12:15, "Looking diligently lest any man fail of the grace of God; lest any root of bitterness springing up trouble you, and thereby many be defiled." Notice this verse begins by saying, "Looking diligently...."The words "looking diligently" are from the Greek word *episkopos*, which is a compound of the word *epi*, which means *over*, and the word *skopos*, which means *to look*. It is from this Greek word *skopos* we get the term for a telescope or a microscope. It's emphasizing that this should not be just a quick glance, but a thorough and precise search.

When you compound the word *epi* and *skopos* it forms the word *episkopos*, which means *to look over, to manage or to give oversight to a thing; to administrate*. It refers to *a supervisory position* and is the New Testament word for *a bishop*. God is calling you to be a bishop, and He's calling me to be a bishop. A bishop? A bishop of what?

Take Responsibility for Your Heart

God has called you to be the bishop *of your own heart*. You cannot blame anyone else for what's going on inside your heart — even if someone else did something wrong to you. You are the only one that has the authority to say *yes* or *no* to strife and offense in your heart. It is *your* heart, and this verse commands you to accept responsibility to be the bishop — *the supervisor* — of your own heart. What goes on in your heart is your business and responsibility to correct. And this verse says to be serious about it — to *look diligently* to bishop and oversee your heart.

Hebrews 12:15 continues: "Looking diligently lest any man fail of the grace of God...." "Grace," the Greek word *charis*, is *an empowering touch that transforms*. But if you're not serious about taking care of your heart, this verse says you're going to "fail of the grace of God." That's a very strange statement. How do you "fail of the grace of God"? Grace is something that God freely does for you. You don't do anything to earn it or to deserve it — God just graces you. So how can you "fail of it?" Here's an illustration that will help you:

Perhaps you're dealing with someone who's very difficult. You've been in strife with them and have become offended. You've prayed and asked God to help you, then suddenly — grace shows up. You're graced! And in that moment, God instructs you how to resolve this relationship. In that moment, you have to take responsibility for your heart and embrace the grace to do the will of God.

If you back up and say, "I know what I need to do, but I'm not willing to do it," the grace that came to help you in your moment of need will become ineffective. That's why we're told by the apostle Paul not to frustrate the grace of God (*see also* Galatians 2:21). God will come to you with grace and empower you to do what you need to do. But if you deny the grace or frustrate the grace, that grace will be in vain; it will be ineffective.

This verse says God's grace will come to help you forgive. God's grace will come to help you resolve the situation, but if you don't accept the grace and partner with the grace you will fail to partake of its sufficiency and supply. If you are not diligent to embrace and apply it, that grace cannot accomplish the magnificent change it was sent to bring in your life and situation.

You'll frustrate the grace of God until it cannot do its job. So James tells us to *look diligently*; to be serious, and to take responsibility for your heart. If you're not taking responsibility for your own heart — to partner with the grace of God — it won't be able to do its job in your life. That's exactly what this verse means.

Hebrews 12:15 continues, "…Lest any *root* of *bitterness* springing up trouble you, and thereby many be defiled." The word "root" is the Greek word *ridza*, and it describes *something that is deeply rooted*. This tells us that bitterness has very long roots. "Bitterness," translated from the Greek word *pikria*, denotes *an inward attitude that is so bitter, it produces a scowl on one's face*. Bitterness has roots so long that not only can it reach from your inner man to your outward expression, but these roots can also stretch from one generation to another generation and to the next.

For example, it may be that some grandchildren never knew the people that hurt their grandparents, yet they're offended by them because the roots of bitterness passed from their grandparents, to their parents, and now have reached them. Some people are offended with entire nations that they've never visited, but a root of bitterness was passed on to them by relatives or friends. Roots of bitterness are very deep. And bitterness always defiles.

We are to be looking diligently, managing our hearts, "…lest any root of bitterness *springing up* trouble you." The words "springing up" are translated from the Greek word *phuo*, which describes *a small plant that pierces its way up through the soil.* The Holy Spirit is telling us to pay attention to what we say, to what we think, and to what we feel. Because when a root of bitterness is working inside us, it will begin to manifest. It will show up as a scowl on our face and a sour attitude in our heart which may cause us to say something sarcastic, caustic, or speak words that are hurtful and sharp. When that root begins to spring up, you need to pay attention to what you are thinking, to what you're feeling, and to the words that are coming out of your mouth.

If you're beginning to speak caustic, sour, sharp words, that is the evidence that there's a seed down deep that's beginning to produce its poisonous fruit. You need to rip it out by the roots before it turns into something terrible. And in fact, the verse goes on to say: "…Lest any root of bitterness springing up *trouble* you" (Hebrews 12:15). The word "trouble" in Greek is the word *enochleo,* which means *to hound, to harass,* or *to stalk.* If you have hounding thoughts of someone, or if thoughts of that person are stalking you and harassing you, provoking bitter thoughts all the time, that is evidence that a spirit of strife and a root of bitterness is working in you.

Sadly, while you're being tormented and troubled with harassing thoughts, the person that you're upset with probably is not bothered at all. Hebrews 12:15 concludes, "Looking diligently lest any man fail of the grace of God; lest any root of bitterness springing up trouble you, and thereby many be *defiled.*" The word "defiled" is the Greek word *miaino,* which means *stained* or *polluted.* It causes something to be *permanently affected.* When a root of bitterness springs up, and a spirit of strife starts to work inside your heart, it will trouble you, and as a result many will be stained and permanently affected by it.

And here's how it happens: You will eventually begin to *speak* what you think about that other person, whether it's true or not. Strife is unreasonable and it provokes negative emotions, stirring up feelings of anger or malice. What you *feel* is what you will *think* about, and that is what you will certainly *talk* about. And when you speak those words in front of others, your bitterness will stain other people's view of that person. As a result, you impart your spirit of bitterness to somebody else. Your friend may not have had a problem at all, but you gave her a problem because you stained that other person's reputation in her eyes. And now every time she hears that person's name or sees that person, her mind is stained with the memory of what you said about that person. You give your spirit of strife and bitterness to other people, infecting them with its horrible pollution, and that's when defilement begins to work in them.

That's what happens when we don't take responsibility for our heart. And that's why we're told to look after it diligently. Sometimes it's hard to forgive; it's difficult to pursue peace. But the Scriptures command us to put on our hunting gear and to make the decision to pursue peace.

In order to pursue peace, we must deliberately put away all weaponized words of strife that would hurt or wound others. We must put away the conflict and begin the process of rebuilding and reconstructing relationships that demon-fueled strife sought to destroy. We must give no place to the devil, but instead give place to the wisdom from above which is pure and peaceable. That's how we'll enter into a time of peace with people. We must seek peace and pursue it until we've captured peace with our spouse, our family, our friends, or our fellow employees.

We need to understand that if we're not willing to do what God asks of us, it will keep us from experiencing His presence. If we don't take hold of the grace of God made available to us, we can end up with a root of bitterness that negatively affects us and others.

But that doesn't have to be your story. Accept the grace of God that will empower you to follow after peace with all men. And if you'll take the initiative to follow after peace, you can close every door to the devil, denying him access to your life. You *can* overcome strife and experience the glorious presence of God and be free indeed!

STUDY QUESTIONS

> Study to shew thyself approved unto God, a workman that needeth not to be ashamed, rightly dividing the word of truth.
> — 2 Timothy 2:15

1. How can you effectively "bishop" or guard and manage your own heart?

2. To do something "diligently" is to do it with conscientious and persistent effort or attention. Hebrews 12:15 tells us to *look diligently,* "…lest any man fail of the grace of God; lest any root of bitterness

springing up trouble you, and thereby many be defiled." What have you learned about applying persistent effort to prevent bitterness and strife?

3.   We are to follow peace and holiness. Describe what that pursuit looks like.

PRACTICAL APPLICATION

But be ye doers of the word, and not hearers only,
deceiving your own selves.
— James 1:22

1.   To pursue peace, you must follow it just as a hunter would follow or chase its prey, then capture it. Read First Samuel 25:2-42, which tells of Nabal, a bitter man, and his wife Abigail, a wise woman who sought peace and pursued it. Her scriptural example demonstrates how to pursue peace and prevent others from being defiled or destroyed by the root of bitterness in another person. Are you willing to go out of your way, despite comfort or convenience, to pursue peace?

2.   The apostle Paul tells us not to frustrate the grace God brings to empower us to repair the destructive results of strife and bitterness. But if we frustrate and resist that grace, it will be ineffective to fix the situation. More importantly, we will remain entrapped by bitterness until we choose to embrace the grace to repent, restore, and reconstruct what was damaged by a devilish intrusion of strife. Have you ever frustrated the grace of God? What was the result?

3.   God has called us to *holiness*, the Greek word *hagios*, which means God has called us to be separate. He has called us to a higher standard and to act differently. It doesn't matter what everybody else is doing; all that matters is what God is asking of us. How are you choosing daily to respond to His higher standard?

Notes

CPSIA information can be obtained
at www.ICGtesting.com
Printed in the USA
LVHW031700220323
742314LV00034B/909

9 781680 319026